KALEIDOSCOPE

THE CONGRESS

by

Suzanne LeVert

BENCHMARK BOOKS

MARSHALL CAVENDISH
NEW YORK

Benchmark Books
Marshall Cavendish
99 White Plains Road
Tarrytown, NY 10591-9001
www.marshallcavendish.com

Library of Congress Cataloging-in-Publication Data.

LeVert, Suzanne.
Congress / by Suzanne LeVert.
p. cm. - (Kaleidoscope)
Includes bibliographical references and index.
Summary: Examines the legislative branch of the United States government, including the process by which a bill is made into a law.
ISBN 0-7614-1451-7
1. United States. Congress-Juvenile literature. 2. Bill drafting-United States-Juvenile literature. 3. Legislation-United States-Juvenile literature. [1. United States. Congress.] I. Title. II. Series.

JK1025.L48 2003
328.73-dc21

2001007570

Photo Research by Anne Burns Images

Cover Photo: Corbis/Adam Woolfitt

The photographs in this book are used by permission and through the courtesy of: *Corbis*: title page;5 The Purcell Team;9 Adam Woolfitt;10,37,38,41 Reuters NewMedia Inc.;13 Lee Snider,14 AFP;30 Wally McNamee;42 Morton Beebe, S.F.; *Jay Mallin*:6,33,34; *Getty Images*:22,25,26;17,18 Newsmakers;21,38 Reuters; *National Archives*:29

Printed in Italy

6 5 4 3 2 1

CONTENTS

A COUNTRY OF LAWS

The United States is a country of laws. The national, state, and local governments make laws that determine how we go about our daily lives—everything from how many days are in a school year to how much in taxes a family pays. Laws that affect the country as a whole, however, are created in Washington, D. C. by the United States Congress. How much the country spends on national defense, what holidays the country celebrates, and how to run national programs such as Social Security and the U.S. Postal Service are just a few of the issues national, or federal, laws address.

Every year on July 4, the United States celebrates its founding. Here, fireworks illuminate the Washington, D.C., skyline, highlighting symbols of our democracy: the Capitol building, the Washington Monument, and, in the foreground, the Jefferson Memorial.

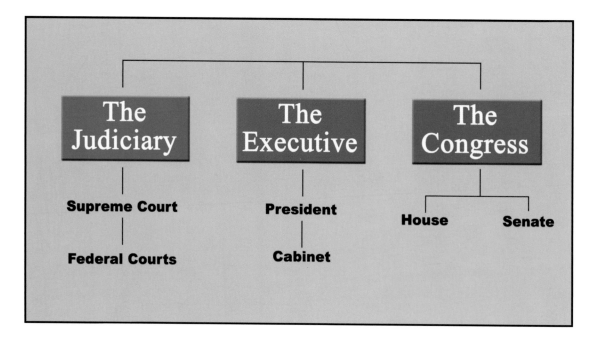

The U.S. Constitution, created in 1787, provides for three branches of federal government. The executive branch, headed by the president, is responsible for seeing that the laws of the country are obeyed. The judiciary branch, headed by the Supreme Court, makes sure that the people of the country—and the world—understand the laws. The legislative branch, called the Congress, creates those laws.

The founding fathers created a system of checks and balances, with three equal branches of government with different duties and responsibilities.

TWO HOUSES OF CONGRESS

Congress consists of two chambers, or houses—the House of Representatives and the Senate. Both chambers meet in the U.S. Capitol building in Washington, D.C. Although the two chambers share many responsibilities, they were created by the founding fathers to meet different needs. The Senate tends to concentrate on issues of national interest, such as defense and international trade. The House of Representatives, on the other hand, brings local- and state-level concerns to the federal government.

The U.S. Capitol Complex, which includes both houses of Congress, congressional office buildings, and three Library of Congress buildings, stands as a monument not only to its builders, but also to the American people and their system of democratic government.

9

The two largest political parties of the United States—the Democrats and Republicans—and other political parties have representatives in Congress. American voters elect members of these parties to office during congressional elections. The party with the greatest number of representatives in each chamber is known as the majority party in that chamber. The other party is called the minority party.

Members of Congress work closely with the president and other members of the executive branch. Here, President George W. Bush meets with Representative Randy Forbes of Virginia in June 2001.

If there are more Democrats than Republicans in the House of Representatives, for instance, the Democrats are the majority party and the Republicans are the minority party. At the same time, however, there may be more Republicans than there are Democrats in the Senate. If that is the case, then the Republicans are the majority party and the Democrats are the minority party in the Senate.

Each state votes to send a certain number of members to the House of Representatives. Today, there are 435 members of the House of Representatives; each member represents, on average, about 572,000 people.

MEMBERS
AND STAFF
ENTRANCE

13

The majority party has more power than the minority party. Generally speaking, the proposals made by members of the majority party are more likely to become laws, because more members of the chamber will vote for than against them. In addition, members of the majority party are chosen to head committees, which are groups of law-makers that concentrate on specific issues. In each house of Congress, each party chooses a majority leader and a minority leader. These leaders help schedule and control the discussion of different proposals that might become laws if a majority of lawmakers vote in favor of them.

The Senate majority leader is elected by his or her peers to lead the party that has the most members in the Senate. The Democrats in the Senate elected Tom Daschle from South Dakota as Senate majority leader in 2001.

15

THE HOUSE OF REPRESENTATIVES

The House of Representatives has 435 voting members from among the fifty states. Each state sends a certain number of representatives to Congress, based on the number of people living in that state. States with large populations have more representatives in Congress than do states with smaller populations. The House also includes several nonvoting representatives from the District of Columbia, Puerto Rico, Guam, American Samoa, and the U.S. Virgin Islands who can discuss issues and suggest new laws.

Puerto Rico, a commonwealth of the United States, sends one nonvoting member—called a commissioner—to the House of Representatives. Here, a mother and daughter celebrate during the Puerto Rican Day Parade in New York City.

Every odd-numbered year, voters in each state elect representatives to serve a two-year term. A member of the House must be at least twenty-five years of age, must have been a United States citizen for at least seven years, and must live in the state he or she represents.

Members of the House of Representatives vote for a leader, known as the Speaker of the House, from the majority party. He or she has many duties and responsibilities. If both the president and vice president die or step down from office at the same time, the speaker becomes president. He or she also rules on procedures that the House must follow, recognizes members who wish to speak during debates, and influences the scheduling of legislation.

The Speaker of the House is elected by members of the majority party in the House of Representatives. Here, Speaker of the House Dennis Hastert, a Republican from Illinois, speaks to the members of Congress in 2001.

The representatives responsible for rounding up votes in support of laws are called whips, and both the majority and minority parties have whips. When members of the House expect a close vote, the whips put together "head counts," or lists of members and how they are likely to vote. The party leadership can then work to convince those members who may be undecided to vote in favor of their party's side of the issue.

Members of Congress work together to enact new laws. Here, Senator Tom DeLay speaks to the Senate membership about legislation involving trade with the country of Cuba.

THE SENATE

The Senate has one hundred voting members, two from each of the fifty states. The term of office for a senator is six years. A member of the Senate must be thirty years of age on the date he or she is elected, must have been a United States citizen for at least nine years, and must be a resident of the state he or she represents.

First elected to the Senate in 1954 at the age of fifty-two, Senator Strom Thurmond of South Carolina became the oldest member of the Senate in 1996 and the longest-serving member in 1997.

The vice president of the United States serves as president of the Senate. In this position, he or she may preside over the Senate and can break a tie vote. When the vice president is not present, an officer called the president pro tempore fulfills that duty. The most important officer of the Senate is the "majority leader," the head of the majority party in the Senate.

Elected in 2000, Vice President Dick Cheney serves under President George W. Bush. Here, he speaks in his official capacity to the membership of the United Nations, of which the United States is a member.

HOW A BILL
IS PASSED

Every year, Congress is responsible for making laws and drawing up policies that affect Americans' lives in a variety of ways. It is Congress that decides how to spend the money the government receives through taxation. Congress can approve laws, called treaties, that govern relations between the United States and other countries. Congress—and only Congress—also may declare war against another country in times of trouble.

Here, President George W. Bush signs a bill that put airport baggage screeners on the federal payroll after the terrorist attacks of September 11, 2001.

The major focus of Congress is the drafting and passage of laws. Laws begin as bills, which are proposals that must go through a specific process before becoming laws. Any citizen of the United States can draft a bill, but only members of Congress can introduce legislation and, by doing so, become the bill's sponsors.

Creating new legislation, known as bills or acts, is the primary responsibility of the two houses of Congress

Seventy-eighth Congress of the United States of America;

At the Second Session

Begun and held at the City of Washington on Monday, the tenth
day of January, one thousand nine hundred and forty-four

AN ACT

To provide Federal Government aid for the readjustment in civilian
life of returning World War II veterans.

*Be it enacted by the Senate and House of Representatives of the
United States of America in Congress assembled,* That this Act may
be cited as the "Servicemen's Readjustment Act of 1944".

TITLE I

CHAPTER I—HOSPITALIZATION, CLAIMS, AND PROCEDURES

SEC. 100. The Veterans' Administration is hereby declared to be
an essential war agency and entitled, second only to the War and
Navy Departments, to priorities in personnel, equipment, supplies,
and material under any laws, Executive orders, and regulations per-
taining to priorities, and in appointments of personnel from civil-
service registers the Administrator of Veterans' Affairs is hereby
granted the same authority and discretion as the War and Navy
Departments and the United States Public Health Service: *Provided,*
That the provisions of this section as to priorities for materials shall
apply to any State institution to be built for the care or hospitalization of veterans.

SEC. 101. The Administrator of Veterans' Affairs and the Federal
Board of Hospitalization are hereby authorized and directed to
expedite and complete the construction of additional hospital facili-
ties for war veterans, and to enter into agreements and contracts
for the use by or transfer to the Veterans' Administration of suitable
Army and Navy hospitals after termination of hostilities in the
present war or after such institutions are no longer needed by the
armed services; and the Administrator of Veterans' Affairs is hereby
authorized and directed to establish necessary regional offices, sub-
offices, branch offices, contact units, or other subordinate offices in
centers of population where there is no Veterans' Administration
facility, or where such a facility is not readily available or accessible:
Provided, That there is hereby authorized to be appropriated the sum
of $500,000,000 for the construction of additional hospital facilities.

SEC. 102. The Administrator of Veterans' Affairs and the Secretary
of War and Secretary of the Navy are hereby granted authority to
enter into agreements and contracts for the mutual use or exchange

THE COMMITTEE PROCESS

After a member of either the House or the Senate drafts a bill, he or she takes it before a special committee organized to investigate the bill. Meetings—called hearings—are held to record everyone's views of the bill, including members of the executive branch, other public officials, and experts on the issue.

After the hearings, if the committee does not act on the bill, the bill dies. The committee may also mark up, or revise, the bill.

During hearings related to specific issues, interested citizens may come before the members of Congress to testify. Here, rock musician Frank Zappa testifies before a Senate committee against legislation that would allow the government to regulate the content of rock music lyrics.

31

If the committee votes to recommend the bill to the whole House or Senate, the committee chairman instructs the staff to prepare a written report. This report describes the purpose of the bill, what effect the bill may have on other laws and programs, what the president thinks of it, and the views of opposing members of the committee. After making it through the committee process, the bill goes before the entire chamber. The full chamber may then debate the bill further before voting to pass or defeat.

Members of either house of Congress can introduce legislation. This bill, introduced in the 107th Congress (the session that met in 2001 and 2002), recognized the contributions to the civil rights movement by Dr Martin Luther King (after his death) and his widow, Coretta Scott King, by awarding them the Congressional Medal of Honor.

H. R. 2723

To authorize the President to award a gold medal on behalf of the Congress to Reverend Doctor Martin Luther King, Jr. (posthumously) and his widow Coretta Scott King in recognition of their contributions to the Nation on behalf of the civil rights movement.

IN THE HOUSE OF REPRESENTATIVES

AUGUST 2, 2001

Ms. McKINNEY (for herself, Mr. LEWIS of Georgia, Mr. PALLONE, Mr. FIL- NER, Ms. LEE, Ms. CARSON of Indiana, Mr. CUMMINGS, Mr. FATTAH, Mr. HASTINGS of Florida, Mr. HILLIARD, Mr. THOMPSON of Mississippi, Mr. PAYNE, Mr. MEEKS of New York, Mr. OWENS, Mr. TOWNS, Mrs. JONES of Ohio, Mr. WATT of North Carolina, Mr. RUSH, Mr. SCOTT, Mr. McNULTY, Mr. CLAY, Mr. FORD, Mrs. CHRISTENSEN, Mrs. MEEK of Florida, Ms. WATERS, Ms. MILLENDER-McDONALD, Mr. DAVIS of Illi- nois, Mr. BRADY of Pennsylvania, Mr. FROST, Ms. NORTON, Mr. ROSS, Mr. SABO, Mr. BONIOR, Mr. JACKSON of Illinois, Mr. KUCINICH, Mrs. CAPPS, Mr. LaHOOD, Mrs. MINK of Hawaii, Mr. McGOVERN, Mr. WYNN, Mr. HONDA, Mr. BLAGOJEVICH, Mr. BARRETT of Wisconsin, Mr. FARR of California, Mr. ETHERIDGE, Mr. DOGGETT, Mrs. CLAYTON, Mr. DeFAZIO, Mr. KILDEE, Mr. SANDLIN, Mr. ENGEL, Mr. GONZALEZ, Mr. NADLER, Mr. JEFFERSON, Mr. CARSON of Oklahoma, Ms. PELOSI, Mr. UNDERWOOD, Mr. GUTIERREZ, Mr. RANGEL, Mr. RODRIGUEZ, Mr. LAN- TOS, Mr. SOUDER, Mr. BECERRA, Mrs. THURMAN, Mr. CONYERS, Ms. BROWN of Florida, Ms. EDDIE BERNICE JOHNSON of Texas, Mr. CLY- BURN, Mr. HOLT, Ms. KILPATRICK, Mr. PASCRELL, Mr. EVANS, Mr. FERGUSON, Mr. VISCLOSKY, Mr. COSTELLO, Ms. SCHAKOWSKY, Mr. CAPUANO, Mr. LaTOURETTE, Mr. GILCHREST, Mr. MEEHAN, Mr. ISRAEL, Mr. SERRANO, Mr. BAIRD, Mr. MATSUI, Mr. GEORGE MILLER of California, Mr. BISHOP, Mr. WATTS of Oklahoma, Mr. SNYDER, Mr. SANDERS, Mrs. MALONEY of New York, Mr. FRANK, Ms. WATSON of California, Ms. JACKSON-LEE of Texas, Mr. LoBIONDO, Mr. GRUCCI, Ms. SANCHEZ, Mr. WU, Mr. CROWLEY, Mr. SHOWS, Mr. GREEN of Texas, Mr. BARCIA, Ms. SLAUGHTER, and Mr. HOEFFEL) introduced the following bill; which was referred to the Committee on Financial Services

THE OTHER CHAMBER

After the full House or Senate passes a bill, the other chamber then receives it and sends it through the same committee and floor-action process. For example, if the House of Representatives passes a bill, then the Senate gets the opportunity to study it as well. The Senators approve the bill, reject it, ignore it, or change it. If they make many changes to the bill, they will send it back to the chamber where it originated (in this example, the house), to get that chamber's approval on those changes.

On the way to becoming law, a bill often is debated and revised in smaller groups of interested legislators, called committees,. Here, a Senate committee meets.

PRESIDENTIAL ACTION

After both the House and the Senate approve the bill, Congress sends the bill to the president, who can either approve the law or veto it. Presidential approval means the bill becomes law. A veto means that the legislation dies. However, Congress can try to "override" the veto.

The president of the United States has the power to veto—or reject—a bill that comes before him from Congress. Here, former President Bill Clinton vetoes the Republican-backed $792 billion tax plan in September 1999.

If two-thirds of both houses of Congress vote to override the veto, the bill becomes law even though the president rejected it. On the other hand, the Supreme Court can "undo" a bill approved by Congress and signed into law by the president. If the justices on the Supreme Court decide that something about the law goes against the Constitution, they can declare the law unconstitutional, or invalid.

As one of the three branches of government, the United States Supreme Court helps to make sure that the laws passed by the Congress and the president conform to the U.S. Constitution. It does this by ruling on cases brought before it involving these laws.

YOUR POWER AS A CITIZEN

Members of Congress are elected to represent all the people of the United States, including you. If you have questions or concerns about how Congress works, or if you see problems in your community that you think need attention, you have a right to talk to your representatives in Congress about them. You can do so by writing to your representatives or senators.

Senators and representatives are elected into office by the voters in their states—and every vote counts! Here, former First Lady Hillary Rodham Clinton campaigns for the office of United States senator from New York, an office she won in 2000.

First, find out the name of your congressperson, then address your letter to him or her like this:

Congressman/Congresswoman (name)
U.S. House of Representatives
Washington, DC 20515

Senator (name)
U.S. Senate
Washington, D.C. 20510

The members of the houses of Congress create the laws that make our country strong and vital. When you reach the age of eighteen, you, too, will be able to influence the way our country runs by voting for the congressmen and congresswomen who shape our nation's present and future.

Our founding fathers created a government "for the people, by the people." Every citizen has a duty to become involved in the issues of the day and to exercise his or her precious right to vote.

GLOSSARY

bill: A proposal to create a new law or change an existing law.

executive branch: The branch of government responsible for enforcing the laws of the nation, made up of the president, the vice president, and other officials.

judiciary branch: The branch of government responsible for interpreting the laws of the nation, headed by the Supreme Court.

legislative branch: The branch of government responsible for creating the laws of the nation, made up of the two houses of Congress—the Senate and the House of Representatives.

majority/minority whip: The whip is the member of Congress who acts as an intermediary between the leadership and the other members of his or her political party in the House or the Senate. The majority whip is from the party with the most members in the chamber.

president pro tempore: The senior member of the majority party in the Senate who serves as the president of the senate when the vice president is absent.

speaker of the house: The presiding officer of the House of Representatives, who is selected by the members of the House.

treaty: An agreement between two nations, such as the United States and Canada.

veto: The rejection by the president of a bill from Congress.

FIND OUT MORE

BOOKS

Jordan, Terry. *The U.S. Constitution and Fascinating Facts About It.* Naperville, IL: Oak Hill Publishing, 1999.

Quiri, Patricia Ryon. *Congress.* New York: Children's Press, 1998.

ORGANIZATIONS & WEBSITES

If you want to see copies of the Constitution, the Bill of Rights, or other documents of national importance, this is the site to check out:

National Archives
700 Pennsylvania Avenue, N.W.
Washington, DC 20408
http://www.nara.gov

This website offers links to every branch of government and lots of other offices and organizations related to the United States government and administrative services:
Thomas: Legislative Information on the Internet
http://thomas.loc.gov/home/legbranch/legbranch.html

You can find addresses of the congresspeople from your state on this website, as well as up-to-date information about what laws the House of Representatives is considering:
U.S. House of Representatives
http://www.house.gov

Find out what's new at the Senate offices and contact the senators from your state at this website:
U.S. Senate
http://www.senate.gov

Suzanne LeVert is the author of nearly a dozen books for young readers on a host of different topics, including biographies of former governor of Louisiana Huey Long and author Edgar Allan Poe. Most recently, she wrote four books in Benchmark Books' Kaleidoscope series on the human body, *The Brain*, *The Heart*, *The Lungs*, and *Bones And Muscles*.

INDEX

Page numbers for illustrations are in boldface.